HORSEMANSHIP
Basics for Beginners

Also by Evelyn Pervier

HORSEMANSHIP

Basics for Beginners

Written and illustrated by
Evelyn Pervier

Photographs by

Melinda Hughes

AN  EQUESTRIAN BOOK

PRENTICE HALL PRESS

New York   London   Toronto   Sydney   Tokyo

Published in 1988 by Prentice Hall Press
A Division of Simon & Schuster, Inc.
Gulf + Western Building
One Gulf + Western Plaza
New York, NY 10023

Originally published by Julian Messner
A Division of Simon & Schuster, Inc.

Previously published by Arco Publishing, Inc.

PRENTICE HALL PRESS is a trademark of Simon & Schuster, Inc.

Library of Congress Cataloging-in-Publication Data
Pervier, Evelyn.
    Horsemanship: basics for beginners.

    Includes index.

    1. Horsemanship. 2. Horses.   I. Title.
SF309.P44 1983   798.2   83-10004
ISBN 0-668-05935-4 (pbk.)

Manufactured in the United States of America

10 9 8 7 6 5 4

For Dick, with love and gratitude

ACKNOWLEDGMENTS

I would like to thank all my friends, young and old, who loaned me their bodies, their horses, and their advice for this book:

Fran Burkell
Andrew and Cassie Burke
Raymond Deiter, V.M.D.
Anne Felix
Ranger Michael Fitzsimmons
Suzie Graeffe
Kate Harling
Samantha Hecht
Paul Hughes
Megan Johnson
Hallie Loring

Ellen Mainenti
Sally Mays
Marion Nelson
Andy Nichols
Dick Pervier
Elizabeth Pickens
Maureen Pinto
Kathy Rohan
Amy Schneider
Bitsy Shields
Jean Wright

CONTENTS

CHAPTER **1**

WHAT IS A HORSE?

CAN YOU IMAGINE an animal so large that he weighs half a ton, yet evolved from a creature no bigger than a small dog? Can you imagine an animal stronger than ten men, yet so fragile he can die if he eats too much rich food? Can you imagine an animal that has lots of hands, yet walks around on giant toenails? Can you imagine an animal that has locks on his knees so that he can sleep while standing up, and can see sideways and backward as well as forward? Can you imagine an animal that has feet and teeth that never stop growing? And an animal that sometimes wears shoes and blankets? This very same creature is the only animal to compete in the Olympic Games. Can you guess which animal it is? Why, the horse, of course!

There is much to learn about this interesting animal, like where he came from and how he evolved. The horse has been a part of the history of humans since the beginning of recorded time, and probably before that. No other animal has played such an important role in human destiny. Down through the centuries the horse has been the partner, servant, and companion of people. He has carried warriors to war, pulled plows for farmers, provided transportation for the masses, and been the inspiration for countless artists and poets.

Let's start at the beginning and trace the origins of this fascinating animal from somewhere in the steamy, prehistoric

The horse. No other animal has played such an important role in human destiny.

swamps of the Eocene period until he evolved millions of years later as the magnificent creature we know today.

THE EVOLUTION OF THE HORSE

Scientists believe the earliest ancestors of the horse (*equus*) first appeared on this planet some sixty million years ago. These small creatures, about the size of a fox, lived in herds that roamed the prehistoric swamps, browsing on leaves. The name given to this early mammal is eohippus.

The eohippus had padded feet, with four toes on the front and three toes on the hind feet. These were defenseless little creatures, having no scales, claws, horns, or fangs with which to defend themselves if attacked. Imagine small herds of the tiny eohippus foraging and browsing through the primeval swamps and woodlands; harmless, peaceful vegetarians grazing warily, forever on the lookout for predators. Even though they could not defend themselves very well, nature had given them large nostrils with which to scent danger, cupped ears to catch the slightest sound, and, most importantly, eyes that were situated on each side of the head that gave them excellent peripheral vision to constantly watch for their enemies and escape by running away.

From studying fossilized remains, scientists believe the eohippus originally inhabited America, southeast England, and western Europe. Gradually, as millions and millions of years passed, the climate of earth changed. Ice ages came and went, land masses broke up forming new continents, and the swampy woodlands became grasslands. Tiny changes took place in the *Equidae* family during this time: the eyes became larger, the hearing more acute, the legs a little longer, giving greater speed. Slowly through the Eocene, Oligocene, Miocene, Pliocene, and Pleistocene periods, the four toes shrank to three toes, and finally to one toe, the hoof. The height of the animal also went from about fifteen inches to

Fig. 1

about five feet. These changes took millions of years, yet somehow the descendants of the eohippus miraculously survived, even though many much fiercer creatures did not. This was because the *Equidae* family was able to adapt itself to its surroundings in a process called evolution. For millions of years these small horses roamed the face of the earth, although they finally disappeared entirely from the American continent. It was not until the sixteenth century that the modern domesticated horse was reintroduced to America by the Spanish, when they won possession of Mexico. Some of the Spanish horses escaped and once again ran wild on the American grasslands. The circle was complete: the horse had returned to one of his original habitats.

THE DOMESTICATION OF THE HORSE

Nobody really knows when the first horses were tamed. Judging by the cave paintings of early people, the horse was originally hunted as prey and eaten. It is thought that sometime around 4000 B.C. nomadic tribesmen first captured, tamed, and rode wild horses. Gradually over the centuries people learned how to select and breed horses for trade, agriculture, and conquest. In Europe heavier horses were developed and used to pull plows and carry soldiers to war. It is important to remember that by comparison with the sixty million years the horse has been on earth, his period of domestication (only about six thousand years) is like a blink of the eye.

THE HORSE'S INTELLIGENCE

Scientists do not consider the horse to be as intelligent as whales or dolphins, pigs or dogs. But like the dog, the horse has a special sensitivity and intuitiveness where people are concerned. This, coupled with an excellent memory and an ability to learn, has made the horse a special partner to humans down through the centuries.

CHAPTER 2

PHYSICAL CHARACTERISTICS OF THE HORSE

NOW THAT YOU know a little more about how the horse evolved, you will be better able to understand his physical characteristics.

Because the horse is a grazing animal (a herbivore), he possesses an elegant, elongated head attached to a long, muscular neck. Like all grazing animals, his eyes are situated on each side of his head, allowing him to see separate images with each eye. To see straight ahead, the horse has to focus the two eyes together. The small, pricked ears can rotate 180 degrees, allowing the horse to listen to sounds all around him. Because the horse is unable to breathe through his mouth, nature equipped him with large nostrils, permitting him to inhale huge quantities of air directly into the lungs. The equine mouth contains a very impressive number of teeth—some twelve incisors, two canines (in males), and twenty-four molars. These teeth grow throughout the animal's life, being constantly worn away as the horse grazes and then grinds the food.

If you look at the profile of an adult horse (See Fig. 2), you will see that his body and legs roughly form a square; the length of the back is approximately equal to the height at the ridge

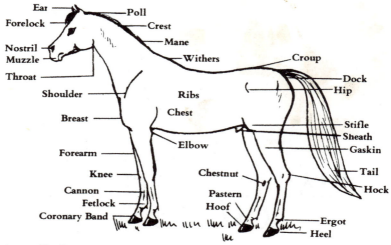

Fig. 2

between the shoulder bones (the withers). The shoulder is long and sloping, allowing for a long, free stride. The chest (the distance from the shoulders to the last rib) is deep, allowing plenty of space for the lungs and heart. The hindquarters are round and powerful; the muscles here propel the horse forward.

Another of the horse's interesting physical characteristics is that he possesses a relatively small stomach in relation to body size. Nature intended the horse to eat small amounts of food almost continuously. Should the horse eat too much food (such as grain) all at once or eat something poisonous, he can become desperately ill and even die because he is unable to vomit.

Compare the horse's front and hind legs with our own arms and legs (See Figs. 3 and 4). Remember that the horse's ancestor, eohippus, was equipped with four toes on the forefeet and three on the hind, but during the process of evolution, all the toes but one disappeared. The modern horse actually walks around on what is really the giant toenail of the one remaining toe. This is called the hoof, and it continues to grow through-

The horse is by nature a grazing animal, a herbivore.

out the animal's life. On either side of the cannon bone are two small bones called splint bones. These tiny bones are the vestigial remains of the toes that disappeared during evolution. On the horse's front leg, what we call the knee is actually the equivalent of our wrist; on the back leg, what we call the stifle is the equivalent of our knee; and the hock is the equivalent of our heel.

Amazingly, the front legs of the horse are not attached to the rest of his body by bones as you might expect but by an incredibly strong harness of muscles. Additionally, the horse's knees contain a locking mechanism, so that the animal is actually able to go to sleep while standing up. After his nap, he unhitches the locks and moves off again.

THE CONFORMATION OF THE HORSE

The term *conformation* means the shape and form of the horse—his physique. Though there are slightly different standards for different breeds, basically the term *good conformation* means that the animal possesses a desirable blend of physical characteristics that makes the overall appearance pleasing and in proportion.

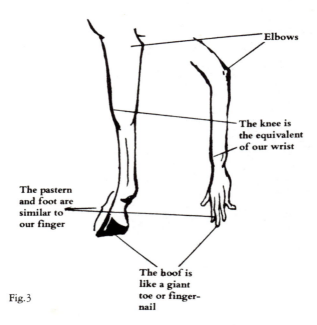

Elbows

The knee is the equivalent of our wrist

The pastern and foot are similar to our finger

The hoof is like a giant toe or finger-nail

Fig. 3

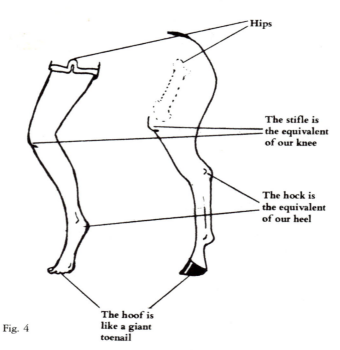

Hips

The stifle is the equivalent of our knee

The hock is the equivalent of our heel

The hoof is like a giant toenail

Fig. 4

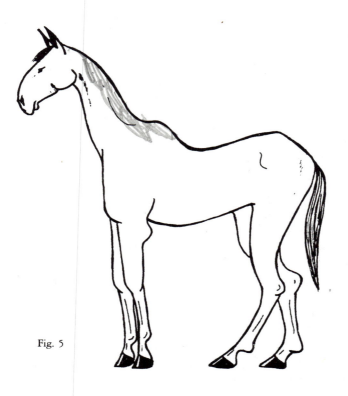

Fig. 5

Even the beginning horseman can soon recognize the dif-
ference between good conformation and conformation faults.
Generally speaking, most horsemen agree that a horse should
have a neat, chiseled head with small pricked ears. Ears that
tend to flop down are called lop ears, and ears too large are
mule ears. If the front of the face is convex-shaped, the face is
called Roman-nosed; if it is concave, it is called dished. The
shape of the horse's neck varies according to breed, but it
should be of medium length and in proportion to the body. If
the topline of the neck is concave, it is ewe-necked. The body
and legs of the horse should roughly form a square. The
shoulder should be long and sloping, giving the horse a long,
free stride; a short or straight shoulder often results in a stiff,

choppy ride. The withers should be reasonably prominent and the back should be short and strong, with plenty of depth to the body. A back that is depressed, or concave, is called swayback, and a convex back is a roachback. The quarters should be round and well muscled, but if the croup slopes sharply down and the tail is set low, the horse is goose-rumped.

Now to the legs. The front legs should be straight, with flat, clean joints and short cannon bones. The pasterns should be of medium length and slant at approximately a 45-degree angle. Short, very upright pasterns are a conformation fault that give an uncomfortably choppy ride. Pasterns that are too long are equally undesirable; the horse is then said to be coon-footed. If you stand in front of the animal and his feet point outward, he toes out. If his feet point inward, then the horse toes in, or is pigeon-toed. If you stand at the side of the horse the legs should present a nice, straight appearance, except, of course, for the pasterns and the hooves. If the knee joint appears to incline backward, the horse is calf-kneed; if the knee buckles forward slightly, he is called over at the knee.

The back legs should be reasonably straight, even allowing for the hocks, with well-muscled stifles and clean hocks. The legs from the hocks down should be vertical until the pasterns, which on the hind legs angle to the hoof at approximately 50 to 55 degrees. If you stand at the back of the horse and his hocks are close together with the feet splayed out, the horse is said to be cow-hocked. When standing at the side of the animal, if the back legs are angled excessively forward under the body, then the horse is called sickle-hocked.

A horse should have good round feet, big enough to support the weight of the upper body. The sole should be somewhat concave, with broad heels and a prominent frog.

Just as there are very few absolutely perfect humans, there are correspondingly very few perfectly conformed horses. Nevertheless, being able to recognize undesirable physical

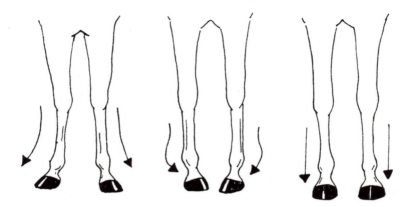

Fig. 6

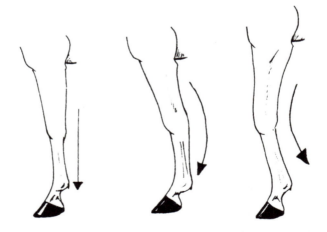

Fig. 7

features enables the horseman to determine the usefulness of the horse. For instance, if you see a horse that appears to be excessively bow-legged (toed in) and compare it with a horse that has straight legs, common sense will tell you which horse has the better, stronger legs. On the other hand, lop ears are not particularly attractive, but they won't necessarily affect the horse's performance. Likewise, small "pig" eyes don't look as beautiful as large, liquid eyes that melt your heart, but they probably do the job just as well. When judging a horse's conformation, the animal should be viewed as a whole with the good points weighed against the faults, with the intended use of the animal taken into consideration. Quite often nature balances undesirable features with other strong points to compensate. Most horsemen can tell wonderful stories about horses that went on to become champions, despite some undesirable conformation faults.

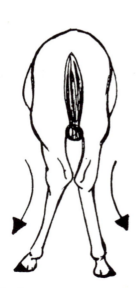

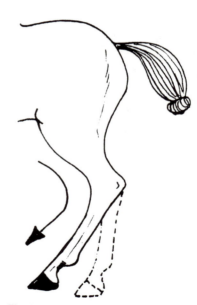

Fig. 8   Fig. 9

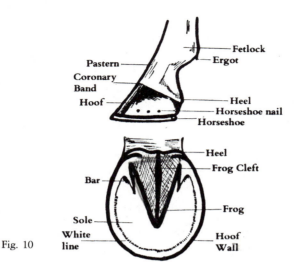

Fig. 10

THE GAITS OF THE HORSE

If you listen to a horse moving on a paved road, you can easily hear the clip-clop rhythmic beat his feet make as they hit the hard surface. Horses have four natural speeds: the walk, trot, canter, and gallop. These are called the gaits, or paces. When we walk, jog, and run, our feet make the sound of two beats, as one leg follows the other: one-two, one-two. Because the horse has four legs, he has to use them in a definite sequence at each pace; otherwise, he could very well trip.

At the walk, the horse lifts up and puts down each leg separately, so we say the walk is a four-beat gait: clip-clop-clip-clop.

The trot is a little harder to understand, because at this gait the animal's feet hit the ground in pairs as the horse springs from one pair of diagonal legs (these are the legs diagonally across his body) to the other pair of diagonals, giving the trot a two-beat gait: double clip-double clop.

The canter is also a little tricky because there are three distinct beats to each canter stride. The horse leads with one shoulder, and both legs on that side of his body (called a lateral pair) hit the ground in advance of the other pair of legs, giving a three-beat gait: clip-clop-clip.

The gallop is an extended form of the canter, only much faster. In this gait the horse puts each leg down separately. This is a four-beat gait, just like the walk: clip-clop-clip-clop.

THE HEIGHT OF THE HORSE

The height of the horse is measured in "hands." Each hand is four inches, and the term is actually derived from the width of a person's hand when, centuries ago, horses were measured by hands placed sideways from the horse's withers to the ground.

CHAPTER **3**

BREEDS AND COLORS

THE EQUINE FAMILY is divided into several different types of horses: the light riding horse, the draft horse (developed to pull heavy loads), the harness breeds (which were used to pull carriages and coaches), and ponies.

A *breed* is a group of horses that all descend from the same source, that are alike in size, conformation, and disposition, and that pass on the same physical characteristics when bred. Here is a description of some of the more popular riding breeds.

The Arabian Horse   Scholars don't know exactly where the Arabian horse originated or when he was first introduced into Arabia. However, long before the birth of Christ, the Arab was the cherished possession of Arabian tribesmen. It is thought that the respect and affection shown by the Bedouins to their horses centuries ago resulted in the wonderful disposition of today's Arabians. The harsh desert conditions also helped create a hardy animal, capable of great speed and endurance. The Arab is one of the soundest of horses, capable of carrying great weight on his short, strong back, which, incidentally, contains one less lumbar vertebra than other breeds. This versatile horse varies in height between fourteen and fifteen hands. He has a small, refined, often dished head, with large

23

The Arabian horse is used extensively in the show ring and for endurance riding. It makes a wonderful pleasure horse for every member of the family.

well-spaced eyes and flared nostrils. His compact body has a short back, with high tail set. He has a slender, arched neck. The legs are elegant and exceedingly strong; the bones of Arabian horses are very dense, resulting in great strength.

Arabs are always a solid color, with white markings found only on the legs and face. They can be bay, black, chestnut, or gray and always with dark, expressive eyes. They are used extensively in the show ring, for endurance riding, and for competitive trail riding, and make wonderful pleasure horses for every member of the family.

The Morgan Horse All Morgan horses descend from one remarkable horse owned over a hundred years ago by a Vermont schoolteacher, Justin Morgan. The horse was named after his owner and was the founding stallion of this important American breed.

Justin Morgan, the horse, was not a large animal by today's standards, standing only fourteen hands high. He was a dark bay with black mane and tail. He probably had Arabian and Thoroughbred blood, but no one really knows for sure.

The Morgan horse. This is Riley of the Mount Tamalpais State Park, making friends while on patrol with his partner, Ranger Michael Fitzsimmons.

He became a legend because he could pull heavier loads than other larger horses, and he won many trotting and running races. The most important contribution of this "little big horse," as he was known, was that his admirable characteristics were passed on to his sons and daughters, no matter what kind of mare he was bred to.

Over the years, the descendants of this amazing horse have increased in size to approximately fifteen hands. They still have the crested neck, short back, and sturdy legs their founder had, plus his admirable qualities of endurance and disposition.

Morgans are used in the show ring and as police horses, cattle horses, trail horses, and even carriage horses.

The Quarter horse is characterized by a small, attractive head, a short back, and a heavily muscled body.

The Quarter Horse   This is the oldest breed of horse in America, and was founded some three hundred years ago during the early Colonial times in Virginia and the Carolinas. In those days it was the custom to hold match races of approximately a quarter of a mile. The horses that became the best of this sport were known as "quarter milers," eventually to be called quarter horses. In the early days the quarter horse was a stocky, short-backed horse of approximately fifteen hands, capable of great bursts of speed if needed. As the pioneers moved south and west, the quarter horse went along too, pulling plows and wagons and herding cattle. Eventually ranchers and cowboys adopted the breed as the perfect "cow" horse. Later, a little Thoroughbred blood refined the breed still further, until today the quarter horse is characterized by a small, attractive head, a short back, and a heavily muscled body. He stands from 14.3 to 16 hands high.

The quarter horse is used extensively as a cattle horse, and in the show ring as a hunter and jumper. He is also used as a racehorse and barrel racer and, because of his pleasant disposition, he makes an ideal family horse.

The Thoroughbred Horse This horse was bred for one purpose: racing. Sometimes people confuse the name Thoroughbred with the term *purebred*. Purebred means the ancestry of an animal (any animal) is pure, whereas the name Thoroughbred applies only to a specific breed of racehorses. These beautiful animals are the most valuable horses in the world, earning millions of dollars for their performances on the racetrack and as breeding stock.

The Thoroughbred breed was established in the late seventeenth century, when three Eastern horses were imported into

The Thoroughbred is used primarily as a racehorse and for breeding purposes, though many are used as hunters, jumpers, event horses, and for dressage.

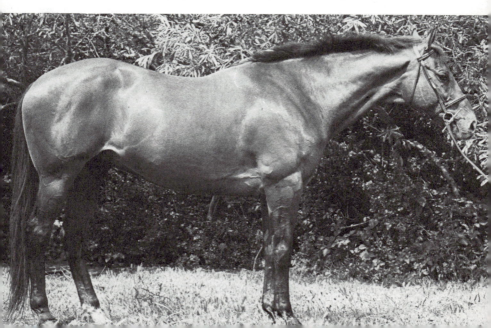

England to improve the homebred British mares. These horses were the Byerly Turk, the Darley Arabian, and the Godolphin Barb—the foundation stones of the Thoroughbred breed. The first Thoroughbreds were quite small, only 14.2 hands high, but gradually as the decades passed, the horses became larger and their speed correspondingly faster.

The Thoroughbred is a refined and elegant animal, possessing a small, chiseled head, a long, lean neck, and sloping shoulders. With plenty of depth to the body he is powered by muscular hindquarters. He stands between fifteen and sixteen hands high and weighs between 1,000 and 1,300 pounds. He can be bay, black, chestnut, or gray with, occasionally, white on face and legs. Because Thoroughbreds are bred primarily for speed, they tend to be more highly strung and temperamental than other breeds.

Though mainly used for racing and breeding, the Thoroughbred also appears extensively in the show ring as a hunter and jumper. Some make excellent field hunters, event horses, polo horses and, occasionally, good trail horses.

The Appaloosa Horse   These spotted horses are the most unusual of all the colored breeds. Throughout early history, pictures of spotted horses appeared in Persia, China, and Spain. In the sixteenth century the Spanish brought colored horses with them when they conquered Mexico. Some probably escaped, some were bartered, and some were probably stolen. At any rate, the Nez Perce Indians in the northwestern part of the United States admired the spotted horse so much that they acquired herds of them, systematically breeding them in an area close to the Palouse River. It is from this river that the name Appaloosa was derived. The Appaloosa coloring appears in four different patterns: the spotted blanket, leopard, snowflakes, and frost. Appaloosas come in all shapes and sizes, but their coloring is extremely consistent as are other distinctive characteristics such as striped hooves, freckled mouths

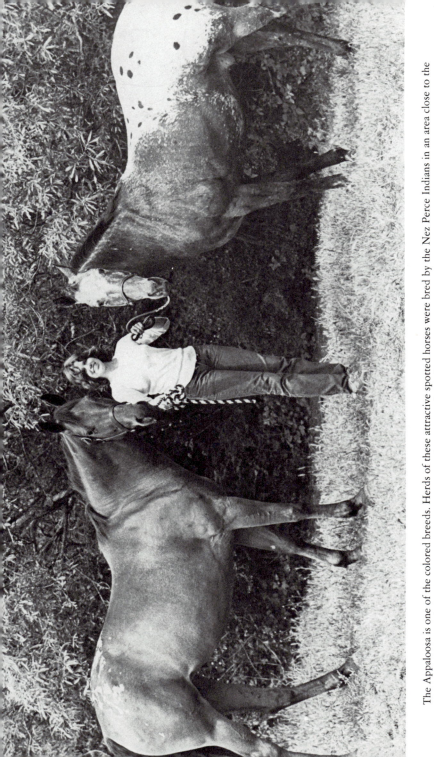

The Appaloosa is one of the colored breeds. Herds of these attractive spotted horses were bred by the Nez Perce Indians in an area close to the Palouse River. It is from this river that the name "Appaloosa" was derived.

The Pinto horse is another of the colored breeds. The coat color is always a combination of white and another color such as bay or chestnut. (*Photo by Fred Curtis*)

and docks, toothbrush manes and tails, and the ring of white (sclera) around the eyes. They are used as ranch horses, jumpers, and racehorses. They also make excellent trail horses.

The Pinto Horse   The pinto (or paint) horse is another of the colored breeds. His coat color is always a combination of white and another color, such as bay, chestnut, or black and comes in two basic patterns: overo and tobiano. Like the Appaloosa, these attractive horses come in different shapes and sizes. Pinto horses are used for ranch work, as trail horses, show and parade horses, hunters, jumpers, and backyard companions.

The Crossbred Horse   This horse is the result of crossbreeding and can be a combination of any breed and type of animal. Most crosses are bred for a particular purpose or specific characteristics. A cross between an Arabian and a Thoroughbred is called an Anglo-Arab, for instance, and the result is an animal somewhat smaller than a Thoroughbred with many of the Arab's admirable qualities of endurance, bone, and even disposition.

The Grade Horse   This is the equivalent of a mongrel in the canine kingdom. The grade horse is simply a combination of so many different breeds and types that no one is sure of his origins.

The Shetland Pony   This is a very popular children's pony that originated on the Shetland Isles, about 120 miles off the coast of northern Scotland. These tiny ponies, the smallest and strongest of the equine family, are thought to have been domesticated three thousand years ago during the Bronze Age.

The Shetland is a gentle, easygoing creature with a small head, neat small ears, and kindly eyes. He has a sturdy, compact body on short legs and stands between twenty-six and forty-two inches high. Sporting a long, shaggy mane and a particularly thick, long tail, a kindly Shetland pony makes an

The Shetland pony has a sturdy body on short legs and sports a long, shaggy mane.

The Welsh pony originally roamed the Welsh mountains. This lovely breed is characterized by a pretty, dished face, attractively agile body, and pleasant disposition. (*Courtesy of Welsh Pony Society of America*)

excellent first pony for a child, as his size is in proportion to the youngster's.

The Welsh Pony   Another of the native British breeds, the Welsh pony has played an important role in teaching children all over the world to ride. For centuries these wild ponies roamed the Welsh hills. It is believed that at some point some Arabian stallions mingled with these herds, resulting in the Welsh pony we see today. This is a pony with a pretty, dished face, attractively agile body, and pleasant disposition. Welsh ponies stand from 12 to 14.2 hands high and are known for their jumping ability, soundness of limb, and attractive "miniature horse" conformation. The Welsh pony is used extensively by both children and small adults in the show ring and in riding schools, and as hunters and trail horses.

COLOR DESCRIPTIONS

If the wild ancestors of the modern horse had been as brightly colored as horses today, it is doubtful that the *Equidae* family would have survived to the twentieth century. Eohippus and his descendants were probably a uniformly brown-gray color, with perhaps a few bars or stripes so that they blended in with their surroundings, just as wild game animals do today. It was not until the horse was domesticated that people were able to selectively breed for color, patches, and spots. Here is a description of some of the most popular colors.

Bay	Reddish brown body, with black mane and tail; usually black lower legs.
Black	True black, without any light areas, even around the muzzle. Mane and tail black.
Brown	Brown body, sometimes with lighter areas around the muzzle, eyes, and inside upper legs. Lower legs usually black, with black mane and tail.
Chestnut	Orange-brown body, with mane and tail the same color or maybe a little lighter.
Dun (or Buckskin)	Beige body, with black lower legs. Black mane and tail. Buckskin has a black dorsal stripe.
Grullo	Mouse-gray body, with black on lower legs. Black or gray mane and tail.
Palomino	Golden-yellow body, with white mane and tail.
Gray	A mixture of white and black hairs, often dappled. The gray horse often starts life with an iron-gray color with black mane and tail; gets progressively whiter with age.
Red Roan	An equal mixture of red and white hairs, which appears reddish in color.
Blue Roan	A mixture of black, white, and sometimes red hairs, which appears bluish in color.

CHAPTER 4

CHOOSING THE RIGHT HORSE

ACQUIRING A HORSE of your own is undoubtedly one of the single most exciting events in a horse-lover's life. It is also a big investment both financially *and* emotionally. You are going to be spending most of your free time with your new four-legged friend and taking on many new responsibilities concerning his care and well-being. Because of this, a lot of thought should go into making absolutely sure that the animal you ultimately decide on is right for you. There are four things to take into consideration at this point: age, disposition, training, and soundness.

Age   The average horse lives twenty-seven years. When he is three or four, he is usually trained, and for a couple of years is considered to be a "green" or inexperienced horse, full of pep and vigor. From the age of six to twelve, the horse is considered to be in his prime. From thirteen through twenty are the mature years, when the horse has lots of experience but none of the foolishness of youth. After the age of twenty, the horse is usually dignified, dependable, and often wonderfully gentle with children.

Disposition   A good disposition (or temperament) is vital and perhaps the most important trait to consider when buying a

Acquiring a horse of one's own is an exciting happening in a horse-lover's life.

horse. Temperament, whether good or bad, is usually inherited and is one characteristic that cannot be altered by training. A bad-tempered, vicious horse will always be bad-tempered and vicious. Fortunately, the majority of horses have pleasant dispositions. Generally speaking, a gelding is usually more even-tempered than a mare.

Training You should know what to expect of a well-trained horse. He should stand quietly as you mount, and walk, trot, and canter when given the correct aids. A young, green horse is rather like a fourth-grader, with plenty of high spirits and not much desire to settle down and work; for this reason the green horse should be avoided by the novice rider. Make sure the horse you are interested in has been trained to perform the particular skill you want. In other words, if you want a jumper, don't buy a barrel racer. As a rule of thumb, the more training a horse has received, the more you must expect to pay for him.

Soundness When you have finally found what appears to be the perfect horse, you should have him medically checked by your veterinarian in what is called a prepurchase examination. If your vet examines the animal but cannot pass him as serviceably sound, don't buy him no matter how disappointed you may be; to do so will only cause you future heartache.

Your horse should be the right size for you. Here the tall rider is riding a pony that is too small for her, while the small rider is riding a Thoroughbred too large for her to handle safely.

WHAT SIZE ARE YOU?

This is an important point to consider. If you are still growing, do not make the mistake of buying a horse or pony that is too small. On the other hand, a small nine-year-old mounted on a sixteen-hand Thoroughbred is riding a horse that is not only too large but also probably too much for the child to handle. Ideally the legs of the rider should extend at least halfway down the sides of the horse so that the rider's leg signals can be felt by the animal.

WHAT IS YOUR RIDING EXPERIENCE?

Answer this one *honestly*! Don't overestimate your riding ability, because the horse will know and will take advantage of you accordingly. If you are a beginner, admit it, for you can only improve. What you need is a gentle, well-mannered horse perhaps in the twelve to twenty age range that will tolerate your early mistakes and at the same time allow you to learn. If you have two or more years of riding experience, then perhaps a well-schooled horse in the prime years of six to twelve is what you need. For a very young child, a docile, elderly animal can be a wonderful babysitter, patiently allowing the child to safely learn rudimentary care and the first steps of riding. There is an old saying that neatly sums up experience: It takes an experienced horse to teach a young rider, and an experienced rider to teach a young horse.

WHAT DO YOU WANT TO DO WITH YOUR HORSE?

Decide which particular riding discipline you are interested in before you buy your new horse. If you just want to go on pleasant trail rides with your friends, then you won't need an expensive, well-trained show hunter. If, on the other hand,

This horse and rider are a comfortable size for each other.

your ambition is to show in jumpers, you should buy a horse that has been trained in this specialty so you won't be disappointed. If you are interested in competitive trail or endurance riding, then an Arabian or Arab-cross would be an excellent choice, having the endurance and durability necessary for this type of sport.

Once you have a firm idea of what kind of horse you want and what you want to do with him, the next step is to find him. Here are some suggestions:

Breeders   If you are looking for a specific breed of horse, then the breeder is an excellent place to start. You can find out the names and addresses of breeders in your area through your local horse associations or through magazine advertising.

Trainers   Trainers invariably know of horses for sale on the show circuit and will quite often go with you when you want to try out a possibility. As long as the trainer is reputable, this is an excellent way for a newcomer to the sport to go horsehunting. Trainers are usually listed in local horse magazines, and your local horse association will probably be able to put you in touch with several trainers in your area. A good trainer will be able to size up your capabilities and, because he or she has a reputation to protect and knows the market, can often find exactly what you are looking for.

Horse Dealers   If you can find a reputable horse dealer—and they do exist—you are in luck. If there is a horse dealer situated near you, make inquiries from clients who have previously purchased horses from him.

Word of Mouth   Tell everyone you know that you are looking for a horse, and let the horsemen's grapevine do its work. Sooner or later you will receive calls from people anxious to sell, and then you can set up appointments and go and look.

CHAPTER 5

STABLING

TAKING CARE OF your new horse is going to be very different from taking care of the family pup. You will need to know what type of accommodations your horse is going to require, what he should eat and how much, and when he should be fed. Let's start with the stabling arrangements. To a large extent your stabling will depend upon a combination of these factors: how much time you have to ride and take care of the animal, where you live, and your budget.

WHAT TYPE OF STABLING IS RIGHT FOR YOUR HORSE?

Your stabling options consist of keeping your horse in a field (pasture), a paddock, a stable, or a boarding facility. Each of these arrangements has its advantages and disadvantages, both for you and your horse. You must weigh each item carefully before making a decision.

Field If you are busy with school or a job and are not able to ride every day, then the most humane way to keep your horse is in a large field, with other horses for company. In this way he can satisfy instincts to graze and exercise. However, a pasture (no matter what the size) is only as good as the feed in it. It can

The most natural way to keep your horse is in a large pasture, preferably with other horses for company.

be two hundred acres, but if the grass is dried up and the nutrition gone, your horse could starve. The answer is to feed the horse additional hay or alfalfa as soon as you notice the grass getting shorter and drier. This will be a must in the fall and winter months.

Another consideration is whether the horse will have adequate shelter to escape from bad weather. A three-sided shelter, a group of trees, or rocks can nicely take care of this, depending upon how the winters are where you live. You must also make sure there is a continual supply of clean water. This will have to be checked frequently, as springs and creeks can dry up and pipes can crack or clog, threatening the life of your horse. Remember, a horse cannot live long without water, especially in hot weather.

Lastly, check the fencing in the area. Walk the fence line to ensure that there are no breaks where your horse could escape or hurt himself. The safest fencing is the wooden post-and-rail variety. Even with this type, however, the boards can split and nails can stick out. Horses very often injure themselves on these projections. If the field is very large, it may be fenced with barbed wire since this is less expensive fencing. However, for horses not used to barbed wire, this can pose quite a problem. They can injure themselves very severely if they become entangled in it. Make sure all barbed wire fencing is tight, and that there are no loose strands of wire hidden in the grass where a horse could catch his foot.

The advantages of keeping your horse in a field are that it is the most natural and the least expensive way to keep him. You also won't have to muck out, and you won't have to exercise your horse on a daily basis. The disadvantages are that you may have quite a walk to catch your animal if the field is large; you may risk a few injuries inflicted either by other horses or the fencing; and you will probably have to supplement the grazing with hay at certain times of the year.

Paddock   If you don't have access to a field, but still want your horse to enjoy as much freedom as possible, then your next alternative is a paddock with a shelter. A paddock is an enclosed area anywhere from an eighth of an acre to an acre or

Check the pasture fence line and re-fence any dangerous places where a horse could become entangled and severely injured in loose, sagging wire.

A paddock with a shelter is a good alternative for your horse if you cannot keep him in a field.

two. Naturally, the larger the better. This type of stabling is particularly suitable in urban areas, provided the local zoning laws permit the keeping of horses. Depending upon the size of the paddock, your horse will be able to walk several miles a day, so you won't have to feel guilty if you cannot ride him every day. You must be sure there is adequate, clean water. The fencing of the paddock is particularly important, and only the best materials should be used. All good fencing is expensive, but as an alternative to the post-and-rail fence, you may want to try electric or pipe fencing or a chain-link fence. Under no circumstances should barbed wire be used in a paddock since the risk of animal injury in such a small area is too great.

Paddock stabling is more expensive than pasture, because your horse is entirely dependent on you for feed and water. A shelter of some kind is also necessary so that the animal may be fed out of the rain, mud, or snow. The horse kept in a small paddock must be mucked out on a daily basis and the manure disposed of. (More on this later in the chapter.)

Stabling a horse in a stall keeps him clean and cozy, but the expense and stable chores are considerable.

Stable (or Stall) Keeping the horse in a stable is probably the most convenient arrangement for the owner. It is the least desirable setup for most horses. Nature intended the horse to be a roaming, grazing herd creature, and life in a stall prevents any of these instincts from being realized. If you plan to keep your horse in a stall, then you must be responsible enough to make sure that he is exercised daily, either by riding or turning him out to play in a paddock. The stall should be at least twelve feet by twelve feet, with plenty of light and plenty of absorbent bedding on the floor.

The advantages of the stable arrangement are that your horse is kept warm and clean in the winter (no scraping off wet mud every time you want to ride); if he is a valuable show animal, you won't run the risk of his being kicked or bitten by other horses; and his coat will stay shorter and shinier all year round because he will not be exposed to inclement weather. One disadvantage is that this is the most expensive way to keep a horse. In addition to your feeding and watering the horse daily, the stall must also be mucked out and rebedded (which is hard work and time consuming); your horse may develop unpleasant stable vices as a result of stall living (weaving back and forth, chewing wood, and wind-sucking, to name a few); and the horse needs to be exercised daily (which can be quite a chore).

Boarding Stable You may not have access to a pasture or room for a paddock or stable in your backyard. Perhaps you don't have the time that is necessary to take care of your horse yourself. Then the solution for you is to place your horse in a boarding stable, where he will be housed and fed for a monthly fee called the board. There may be several boarding stables in your area; visit each one. Make notes and compare the services and facilities offered. Look at the condition of the buildings, the stalls, and, particularly, the horses. Is there plenty of hay in the barn, and does it smell fresh and sweet? Is there plenty of bedding in the stalls, and are the stalls cleaned daily? Is there a locked tackroom where you can store your equipment? Is there an indoor arena, so that you can ride in bad weather? Does the stable have access to riding trails? Do the veterinarian and the farrier (horseshoer) come on a regularly scheduled basis? Is there a mandatory worming and vaccination program? Is there an in-house trainer, so that you can take lessons if you wish? Will the staff turn your horse out for you on a daily basis? Talk to people who already board horses at the stable. They will usually be happy to tell you the good points and some of the not-so-good points of the stable.

When you find a stable that provides the services and facilities you want, make sure that you are a responsible boarder, that you pay your board on time, and that you conduct yourself in accordance with the stable rules.

A FEW WORDS ABOUT MUCKING OUT

If you keep your horse in a paddock or stable, then mucking out will be a daily chore. Horse droppings are usually full of

Mucking out a paddock shouldn't take more than fifteen minutes a day. All you need is an apple-picker and a cart.

parasites eliminated by the horse. Because fresh manure attracts flies, which in turn annoy you and your horse, and because failure to remove manure can result in a variety of unpleasant ailments, particularly one called thrush, which affects the horse's feet, mucking out must be done daily.

If your equine friend lives in a paddock, then mucking out is relatively simple and should not take more than fifteen minutes a day, even if you dawdle. All you need is a tool called an apple-picker, which is a many tined fork (usually available at your local tack or feed store), and a wheelbarrow, cart, or basket (a two-wheel garden cart is good because it doesn't tip over). The average horse deposits approximately sixteen piles of droppings in a twenty-four-hour period. All you have to do is pick these up with your apple-picker and dump them in your cart or basket. Now you need a manure pile or a manure pit to dispose of your load.

If you choose to dig a manure pit so that your manure is not

Mucking out a stable takes longer because you have wet bedding as well as manure to contend with.

visible, it should be about three feet deep and approximately three feet wide by seven feet long, with a matching ventilated cover (easily made from a piece of four-by-eight-foot plywood, with holes cut in it). Both a pit or a pile should be situated well away from your house and your stable, yet with easy access for daily use and periodic removal. The manure will steam when stored in a stack or pit. There is no cause for alarm. This is a perfectly natural biological function caused as the manure breaks down and composts, generating heat as it does so.

Mucking out a stable takes a little longer and is a bit more strenuous because you have wet bedding to contend with in addition to the droppings. If you use straw as a bedding, you will need a four- or five-tined pitchfork. Rake and stack the clean straw in one corner, and lift out the wet straw and all the droppings and deposit them in your cart. Allow the floor to air a little and rebed with the straw you saved. Then add sufficient new straw to make a thick, comfortable bed. If you use shavings as bedding, basically the same rules apply, but the apple-picker is a handier fork to filter the droppings from the shavings.

CHAPTER **6**

FEEDING THE HORSE

WHEN YOU SIT down to enjoy your evening meal, it probably contains half or maybe all of your daily nutritional requirements. You can eat this meal in less than fifteen minutes and suffer no ill effects. But nature designed the horse to eat his daily nutritional needs *slowly*, over the course of twenty-four hours. If your horse tried to eat most of his daily nutritional requirements all at once, he could easily become desperately ill. His stomach is relatively small and can only digest small amounts of food at a time. When the horse is eating naturally in a pasture, he grazes. Then he rests and grazes some more

The horse's menu consists of grass or good quality hay, supplemental grain if necessary, a trace mineral salt block, and fresh clean water available at all times.

throughout the day. In the process he may take in small amounts of grain if the grasses happen to be in seed. When we put our horse in an environment where he cannot graze, such as a paddock or a stall, we have to find a substitute for the fresh, green grass he prefers, a substitute that will take several hours to consume so that his instinct to eat on and off throughout the day will be satisfied. The answer is hay, the horse's roughage.

WHAT TO FEED

Depending on where you keep your horse, his menu will consist of combinations of the following:

- Pasture, with supplemental hay and/or grain, if necessary.
- Hay (instead of pasture).
- Supplemental pellet, grain, or bran rations, if necessary.
- Trace mineral/salt block, available at all times.
- Fresh water, available at all times.

Hay should always smell sweet, be bright in color, and be free of dust, mold, and weeds. Buy it only from a reputable feed store or hay dealer, who will promptly replace any bales that appear suspect when opened. Moldy hay can kill your horse, and so can certain weeds (such as fiddleneck and yellow-star thistle) if eaten in sufficient quantities. There are basically three different types of hay: legume hay (alfalfa and clover), grain hay (oat), and grass hay (timothy and rye). Nutritionally, alfalfa is superior to oat hay, which is in turn superior to timothy. To a large extent, the kind of hay you feed your animal depends upon where you live. In the East, it is sometimes impossible to obtain good-quality alfalfa, so oat and/or timothy hay are used instead. Because grass hays do not contain sufficient protein and calcium, your horse will have to also be fed a grain or pellet ration, depending upon the amount of daily work he does.

HOW MUCH SHOULD YOUR HORSE
EAT EVERY DAY?

The average horse of approximately 1,000 pounds, ridden lightly, should eat about twenty pounds of hay a day, divided into two feedings of ten pounds in the morning and ten pounds in the evening. This translates into 600 pounds a month, or 3½ tons of hay per year per horse. Any supplemental pellet or grain rations you may want to feed your horse should be divided up and given in small quantities after the horse has eaten some hay so that the edge is taken off his appetite. In this way, he won't bolt the grain. Allow the horse at least an hour to digest grain feeds before attempting to work him. The wisest course is to ask your veterinarian to give you a feeding program; he or she will be familiar with the type and quality of feed available in your particular area.

Horses thrive on routine, so always feed your horse at the same time morning and evening.

WHEN TO FEED

Horses thrive on routine, so feed yours at the same time every morning and evening. If your friend expects his breakfast at 8 A.M., and you are still snuggling in your bed, he's going to be very upset. The result of this distress can cause him to kick the stable door to get your attention, to whinny frantically, and to generally misbehave. So, set up a routine and stick to it, no matter how late you partied the night before. You will be rewarded with a healthy, happy horse.

HEALTH CARE RELATED TO YOUR FEEDING PROGRAM

All horses are subject to internal parasites we horsepeople call worms. There is no way to completely eliminate these pests, but by having your veterinarian *regularly* worm your horse, you will at least keep the numbers down. Internal parasites can cause a wide variety of ailments, from loss of weight and poor coat condition to colic (severe gastric disturbance) and even death. Because the worms indirectly eat the food you give

There is no way to completely eliminate internal parasites, but having your veterinarian worm your horse on a regular basis will at least keep the numbers down.

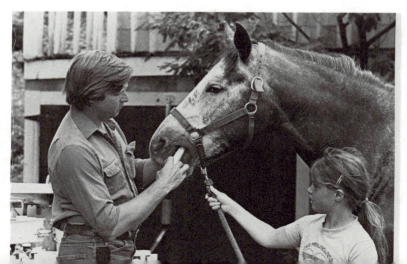

Your horse should be regularly vaccinated to protect him from a host of deadly diseases.

your horse, it makes good sense economically to kill the worms so that your horse keeps the benefit of the expensive nutrition you give him.

Your veterinarian will also be able to vaccinate your horse for protection from a host of unpleasant and sometimes deadly diseases, such as tetanus, rabies, equine influenza, and rhinopneumonitis. Your vet will also want to check your horse's teeth on a regular basis, and if necessary "float" them with a rasp to even them out. Many horses have problems with long, sharp teeth and lose condition rapidly if the problem is not rectified. (NOTE: Health care is covered more comprehensively in *Horsemanship: Basics for Intermediate Riders*.)

CHAPTER 7

GROOMING

HORSES LIVING TOGETHER in a field or paddock can often be observed standing head to tail, itching each other with their teeth, obviously enjoying the experience. This kind of grooming is apparently an important part of equine herd life. When you groom your horse or pony, you simulate this function, but you also do much more. Grooming gives you the opportunity

Horses often groom themselves by itching each other with their teeth.

Tie the horse approximately 2′6″ from the rail, using the quick-release slipknot shown in Fig. 11.

Never tie a horse by the neck; he may choke.

to thoroughly check out your animal's body on a regular basis, noting any small wounds, itchy places, or parasites he may have picked up (more on these pests later). Regular grooming promotes condition and keeps your horse's pores from being clogged with dirt and sweat. As a result of your diligence, you will be rewarded with a healthy, glossy coat on your horse.

FIRST YOU MUST TIE YOUR HORSE

Use a nylon halter and lead rope and tie your horse to a *secure* rail, pipe, or hitching post. Tie the horse approximately 2½ feet from the rail, using the quick-release slipknot shown in Fig. 11.

- *Never* tie a horse by his neck; he may choke.
- *Never* tie a horse by the reins; if he pulls back, the bit may severely cut his mouth; also, the reins may break.
- *Never* tie a horse to a flimsy object; if he pulls back, the object will invariably break and frighten him even more.
- *Never* tie a horse too long; his legs can get tangled, causing rope burns or even broken bones.

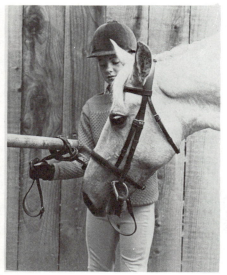

Never tie a horse by the reins; if he pulls back, the bit may cut his mouth. Or the reins may break.

Never tie a horse to a flimsy object; if he pulls back, the object is pulled along, frightening him even more.

Never tie a horse too long; he may get his legs tangled in the excess rope, causing rope burns or even broken bones.

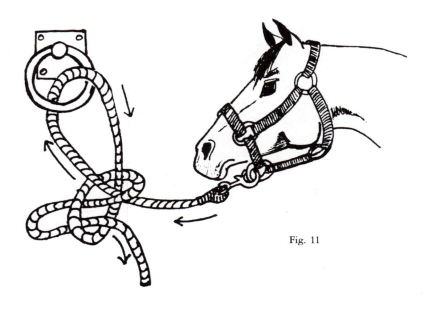

Fig. 11

GROOMING TOOLS AND ITEMS YOU WILL NEED

Tack Box	May be a wooden or plastic box with a handle, or a large bucket; used to hold all your grooming necessities.
Dandy Brush	Used to remove heavy dirt and mud.
Body Brush	Used to remove dust and to polish the coat.
Rubber Grooming Glove	Used to remove scurf and dust from the coat and to promote circulation by massaging the skin.
Rubber Curry	Used to clean dirt and mud from the coat and also to clean other brushes.
Water Brush	Used to dampen and brush the mane and tail and to clean the feet.

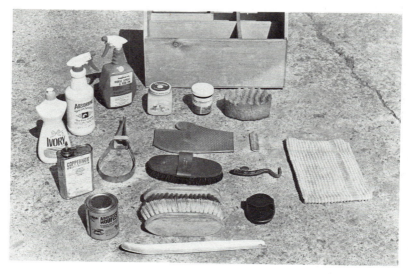

Grooming tools and items you will need.

Sponge	For sponging around eyes, nostrils, and the area under the tail (the dock); also for bathing.
Hoof Pick	For picking dirt and rocks from the hooves.
Shedding Blade	Use the serrated edge of this blade to remove loose hair from the coat.
Sweat Blade	Use the smooth side for removing sweat and water from the coat when animal is washed.

All your grooming tools and items should be marked with your name and kept in a tack box.

Mane Comb	Used for pulling (thinning) the mane.
Fly Spray	To prevent flies from annoying you and your horse.
Antibiotic Ointment	For small abrasions.
Vaseline	For smaller abrasions.
Kopertox	For the bottom of the feet to prevent thrush.
Hoof Dressing	For the walls of the hoof.
Mild Soap	For occasional bathing.
Hair Conditioner	For the tail to remove tangles.
Towel	For polishing, wiping, rubbing, etc.

All these items should be marked with your name and kept in your tack box. It's also a good idea to frequently wash all your tools and your towel with a disinfectant soap.

GROOMING

Start at your horse's neck, and with your dandy brush or rubber curry, give his entire body a going-over, using short hard strokes and circular motions until all the heavy dirt and mud are removed. Now do the same thing all over again with your rubber grooming glove or your body brush. If it is summertime and your horse's coat is short, you won't need to use your dandy brush at all. You can start right in with the rubber grooming glove and the body brush. Incidentally, brush your horse hard enough to penetrate through the coat to the skin below, but be careful around sensitive parts such as eyes, nostrils, dock, and girth. When you have finished the body, carefully brush the face with the body brush. Next dampen your water brush and brush the mane and tail, taking care not to break the hairs of the tail as you remove tangles. If your horse

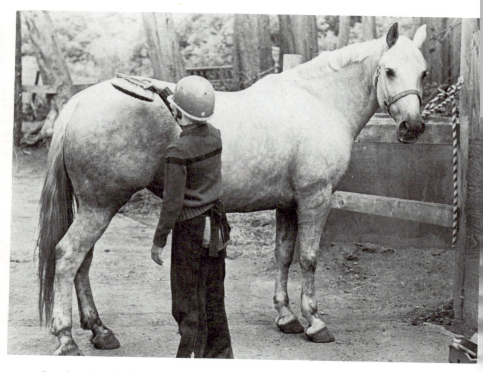

Start by giving the horse's entire body a going-over with your dandy brush.

has a very tangled tail, shampoo it with a mild shampoo, rinse, and then rub on some human hair conditioner. When the tail is dry, carefully untangle the knots with your fingers, and finally *brush* it out. Never comb a tail. This breaks too much hair and will quickly shorten a long tail.

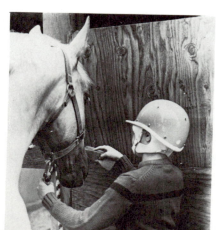

You can clean the nostrils with a damp sponge.

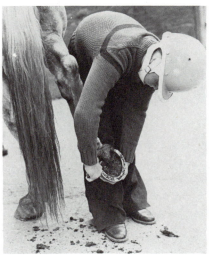
Cleaning out the feet.

CLEANING THE FEET

Stand at your horse's shoulder and face his tail. Now pick up the front foot by running your hand down the back of his leg and leaning slightly against his shoulder. Cup the foot in one hand and clean out any debris that has collected in the bottom of the hoof (See Fig. 10) and around the frog, using your hoof pick. Repeat this procedure for all four feet, always standing at the side and facing the tail. In this way, if your horse should kick at a fly or move suddenly, you won't be in any danger. Once a week—and more often in wet weather—squirt Kopertox all over the frogs, heels, and soles of your animal's feet to prevent a disease of the frog called thrush.

A FEW WORDS ABOUT EXTERNAL PARASITES

Generally speaking, there is no cause for alarm if you occasionally see something make a home in your horse's coat. The chances are that your horse has probably picked up a tick (a blood-sucking parasite) while you were out riding. Simply pick

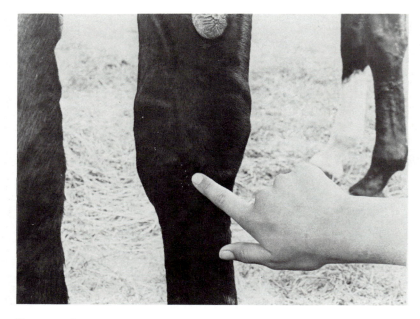

You can easily remove the yellow bot fly eggs yourself by carefully scraping the hairs with a razor blade or a bot knife.

it off by twisting and pulling, stomp on it, and forget it. Owners sometimes find that their horse has suddenly acquired a host of pests, such as chiggers, lice, or ticks. If this happens to your animal, call your veterinarian immediately and ask him to identify the parasite. He will probably give you a chemical dip to apply to the coat.

There is one pest you can easily take care of yourself. The bot fly, which looks like a large bee, lays its yellow eggs on the hairs of a horse's coat. You can remove these yourself by carefully scraping the hairs with a razor blade or bot knife. Be sure to remove these eggs as soon as you see them, before your horse ingests them (by licking the coat) and they start their damaging life cycle internally.

CHAPTER 8

TACK AND TACKING UP

FOR AS LONG as humans have been riding horses, a harness (or tack) has been used as a means of controlling the animal. For hundreds of years there have been very few changes in the basic needs: a bridle to hold the bit in the horse's mouth and reins so that the rider can turn and stop; a saddle, held on with a girth, with stirrups giving the rider the freedom to move around in the saddle without losing balance. As a beginning horseman, you should try to keep your tack requirements as simple as possible. All you really need is a snaffle bridle and an all-purpose saddle. All tack buckles up on the left side. This is called the horse's near-side. The right side is called the off-side.

Snaffle Bridle   A bridle is named for the particular bit it carries; thus, a snaffle bridle carries a snaffle bit. The snaffle is the mildest of all bits, and the one with which the beginner can do the least amount of damage to the horse's tender mouth. The bridle itself consists of several leather straps that hold the bit in the horse's mouth with reins that lead from the bit to the rider's hands.

All-Purpose Saddle   This is a useful saddle for the beginner and one that will allow the rider to practice various disciplines such

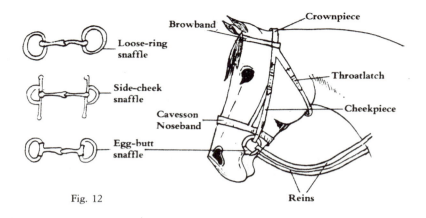

Loose-ring snaffle
Side-cheek snaffle
Egg-butt snaffle

Browband
Crownpiece
Throatlatch
Cavesson Noseband
Cheekpiece
Reins

Fig. 12

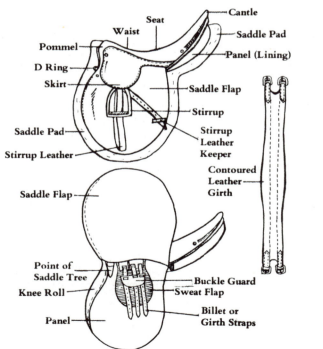

Seat
Cantle
Waist
Saddle Pad
Pommel
Panel (Lining)
D Ring
Skirt
Saddle Flap
Stirrup
Stirrup Leather Keeper
Saddle Pad
Stirrup Leather
Contoured Leather Girth
Saddle Flap
Point of Saddle Tree
Knee Roll
Buckle Guard
Sweat Flap
Panel
Billet or Girth Straps

Fig. 13

as jumping, trail riding, or elementary dressage. This saddle places the rider in the central, lower part of the seat, over the horse's center of gravity.

Saddle Pad Usually made of nylon or felt and placed under the saddle to prevent friction and to absorb sweat.

Girth Used to attach the saddle securely to the horse's back. The best girths are usually made of leather and come folded or contoured. Some have elastic straps at one end.

Stirrup Leathers These hold the stirrups and hang from the stirrup bars of the saddle. They are adjustable so that the stirrup may be lengthened or shortened, depending on the rider's height.

Stirrup Irons Should be made of stainless steel and should fit your foot width, allowing at least half an inch clearance on each side of your boot. Most stirrups come equipped with rubber stirrup pads to give your foot additional traction. Note: Stirrups are run up the back of the leathers to the stirrup bars when the saddle is being carried, placed on or off the horse's back, and when stored.

TACKING UP

Start with the saddle, so that your horse's sensitive back can be warming up while you finish your preparations. Stand on the horse's left, or the near-side, and place your saddle and the pad over the withers. Now slide both into place in the hollow just behind the withers. Make sure your pad is lying flat under the saddle. Now take your girth and quietly go to the horse's off-side and attach it. It should hang down immediately behind the elbow. Go back to the near-side and reach down, catch the girth, and buckle it up *loosely.* Gently ease the saddle pad up under the pommel, so that air can circulate and the withers are not "bound" by the pad.

Now for the bridle. This is a little trickier. Some horses seem to realize when a beginner is learning how to bridle and deliberately hold their heads as high as possible to thwart all attempts. Keep a sense of humor—and keep practicing.

First make sure the noseband and throatlatch are unfastened. Then place the reins over the horse's head. Now unbuckle the halter and rebuckle it around the neck like a dog collar. Hold the bridle with one hand halfway up in front of the horse's face and gently guide the bit into his mouth with the other hand. Raise the bridle and ease it gently over the ears. Once the bridle is on, straighten out the noseband and the browband. Lastly, fasten the throatlatch loosely and the noseband firmly.

Return to the saddle and gently tighten the girth, making sure you have not pinched the sensitive skin behind the elbows. Unbuckle your halter, and your horse is ready to be led away. You may lead him either by taking the reins over the

When saddling up, stand on the horse's near-side and place the saddle over the withers; then slide it back into the hollow just behind the wither.

Next, buckle up the girth loosely. It can be tightened up just before you mount.

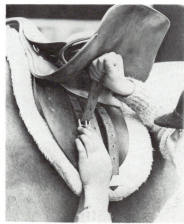

To bridle the horse, hold the bridle midway up the face with one hand and slip the bit between the horse's lips with your other hand.

Ease the bridle gently over the horse's ears.

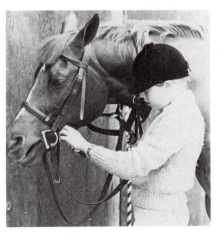

Then straighten out the noseband and fasten the throatlatch.

head and holding them on the near-side, as if they were a lead rope, or by simply holding the rein on the near-side just behind the ring of the snaffle bit.

CHAPTER 9

MOUNTING AND RIDER POSITION

SAFETY FLASH! Remember to wear your hard hat every time you mount and ride a horse.

Before mounting, the first step for the new rider is to gauge the length of stirrup required in relation to height. To do this, pull the stirrup down to the bottom of the leather. Tuck it under your armpit and try to touch the stirrup bar with your finger tips. Your leg in the stirrup will be roughly the same length, so you may adjust the leather up or down accordingly.

Step two is to check your girth once again and retighten it if necessary. Now you are ready to mount your horse.

Mounting Stand by your horse's near-side shoulder, facing the tail. With your left hand, gather up the reins evenly (so that your horse can't leave without you), take a little mane, and rest this hand just in front of the withers. With your right hand, pull the stirrup toward you and put your left foot in it, so that it is pointing toward the tail. Now for the hard part. With a hop, grasp the back of the saddle (the cantle), pull yourself up, swing your leg over the back, and sit yourself down gently in the saddle. Put your right foot in the right stirrup, and con-gratulate yourself. You did it. With just a little practice you

Remember to wear your hard hat every time you mount and ride a horse.

How to tell the correct length of stirrup in relation to your height.

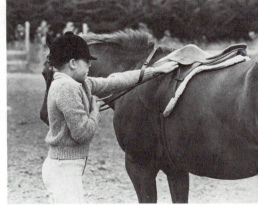

To mount, stand facing the tail and holding the reins with your left hand. Pull the stirrup toward you and put your left foot in it.

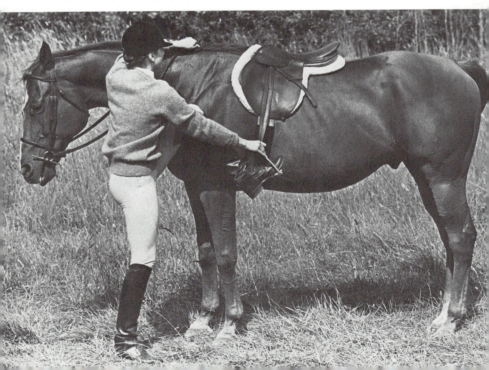

Swing yourself up . . .

. . . and over.

will be able to improve your technique, so that you can mount in one graceful, fluid movement.

If you are small and attempting to mount a very large horse, try lengthening the stirrup leather on the near-side some six or eight inches, so that you don't have to stretch up so far with your leg. Once you are in the saddle, you can easily shorten your leather to the correct length, but don't forget to hold your reins while you do so. Another mounting aid is the mounting block. You can use a sturdy wooden box as a substitute. Just lead your horse alongside the box and mount in the usual way.

Dismounting This is easy! Kick *both* feet out of the stirrups, hold your reins in your left hand, lean forward, and slide off on the near-side by swinging your right leg over the back of the horse. To prevent jarring your legs when you land, bend your knees slightly as you jump to the ground. When you have landed safely, control your animal by holding the reins just behind the bit on the near-side.

RIDER POSITION

Study the photograph demonstrating the basic rider position and try to fix it in your mind's eye so you can emulate it when you are in the saddle.

Your head should be up with your eyes directed over the horse's ears. Your shoulders should be back, and you should try to square them up with the horse's shoulders. Allow your arms to hang naturally from your shoulders, but bend them at the elbow to form a straight line between your lower arms, hands, and reins to the bit. Hold a rein in each hand, passing it between your third and fourth fingers, across your palm, and out between your first finger and thumb. The reins should be held just above the withers, three inches up and three inches apart.

Now to your legs. Try to keep a light, natural contact with

The rider's position.

How to hold the reins correctly.

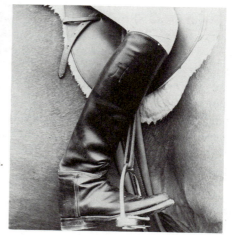

The correct leg position.

the horse using your inner thigh, knee, and calf. Your lower leg should be back a little behind the girth. Heels should be down (pretend you have heavy weights in them), and the balls of your feet should rest in the stirrups. Point your toes forward and slightly out.

Here is a quick rundown of some of the basic equitation terms and what they mean.

The Seat   really has two meanings:

1. The part of your body next to the horse's body, including your lower back, pelvis, and the insides of your thighs and calves.

2. Your position in the saddle, depending on your riding activity. For example, jockeys ride with extremely short stirrups perched over the horse's neck in a racing seat. Hunters ride with medium-length stirrups in a forward seat. Dressage riders use longer stirrups, sitting tall and deep in the saddle in a dressage seat.

The Hands   We guide and control the horse with our hands when we ask him to start, stop, turn, or halt. "Good hands" are hands that sensitively communicate instructions to the horse via the reins.

The Aids   These are signals, a sort of sign language between the horse and rider, telling the horse what we wish him to do. These aids can be either natural or artificial. The natural aids are the parts of the rider's own body such as hands, seat, legs, and even the voice. The artificial aids are pieces of equipment, such as the whip and spur, used to complement or accentuate the natural aids.

Transitions   are rather like gear changes in a car. They are changes in the gaits from the walk, to the trot, canter, and gallop and back down again to the canter, trot, walk, and halt.

CHAPTER **10**

LEARNING TO WALK, TURN, AND HALT

THE WALK IS your first introduction to moving your body in unison with the rhythm of the horse. Once mounted, sit in the basic rider position previously described. Pick up your reins quietly so that you have light contact with the mouth. Apply enough pressure with your legs to the horse's sides so that he gets your message and starts to move forward. Encourage this forward momentum by driving (pushing) with your seat. Allow your hands to follow the back-and-forth movement of the horse. If your horse is a little lazy about responding to the aids you have given him, try a verbal aid like clucking. Once you are walking along at the speed you want, relax your leg pressure and concentrate on moving to your horse's rhythm.

TURNING

Most of the aids you communicate to the horse about turning come from your seat and legs, with the hands regulating the angle of the turn. Before you do anything, you must anticipate the turn in advance with your eyes, and then allow the horse plenty of time and room to respond. After all, you know where you wish to turn; your horse does not. If you wish to turn to the left, put your left leg against the girth, and your

The walk, with the rider in the basic rider position.

Turning or bending around a corner. Notice the rider anticipating the turn in advance with his eyes. His left leg is held firmly against the girth, with his right leg behind the girth. He is squeezing the left rein to guide and regulate the turn, while maintaining light contact with the outside rein.

right leg behind the girth. Squeeze the left rein to the left, but at the same time, maintain contact with your right rein. Try not to jerk or haul on the horse's mouth as you turn the corner; keep your movements quiet and subtle. Once you have turned your corner, discontinue your turning aids and resume walking. For a right turn, reverse this procedure.

HALTING

In the halt, you are going to ask your horse to "listen" to your seat by first bracing your back and then pushing your seat bones down and forward into the saddle. Keep your chin up and do not look down—a huge equitation fault. Close your hands on the reins, so that there is no more give in them. When your horse halts, relax your hands, seat, and legs.

CHAPTER **11**

LEARNING TO TROT

THE TROT IS a springier, faster gait than the walk, and at first it is quite difficult because the horse springs from one pair of diagonal legs to the other. As a result, you may find that your body refuses to cooperate with you, leaving you lurching about insecurely in the saddle. But if you persevere and concentrate on the rhythm of the trot, you will eventually get it. There are two ways of riding the trot: sitting and posting.

The Sitting Trot　This is ridden with shoulders back and head held high, in the basic rider position. Shorten your reins slightly, push with your lower back, and squeeze with your legs until the horse is trotting at the speed you want. Your seat is supposed to stay *in* the saddle at the sitting trot, so relax your pelvis, thighs, and calves and try to imagine that you have huge anchors attached to each heel, holding you down securely in the saddle.

The Posting (or Rising) Trot　For the posting trot, you are going to change your basic position from upright (as in the walk and sitting trot) to a slightly forward position. You are also going to learn how to post: to rise and fall as the horse moves from one pair of diagonals to the other. Shorten your reins and squeeze with your legs until you are trotting. Now

In the sitting trot the rider sits tall, with his seat *in* the saddle.

count the beats one-two, one-two, and try to post up and down with the motion allowing the horse's movement to propel you up and slightly forward, and then gently down again. Here are some hints to help you perfect your posting trot.

- Try not to "pump" by rising too high and upright in the saddle, as this makes you thump down on the horse's back, encouraging him to go even faster, thus increasing your discomfort.
- Fasten a spare stirrup leather around your horse's neck (called a neck strap) and hold on to it for support as you practice. This will help steady you as you learn to post

The posting trot. In this gait, the rider's body is inclined forward a little and his reins correspondingly shortened. The rider is demonstrating the correct diagonal as he raises his seat out of the saddle as the horse's outside (rail) leg is lifted.

and will keep your hands quieter so that you will not inadvertently jab your horse's mouth.
- Look up and in the direction you are trotting.

LEARNING YOUR DIAGONALS

If you are a beginner, you may have heard other riders talking about right or wrong "diagonals," but to you, diagonals are just a big mystery. To understand what diagonals are, you must first think of the horse trotting in a circle; when working in a curve, the outside of his body has to travel a little farther than the inside. The rider assists the horse to balance around the circle by lifting his or her weight *out* of the saddle when the horse lifts his *out*side front leg.

How do you accomplish this quite complicated feat? Sit the trot for a few steps and glance down (moving your eyes only, not your whole head) at the horse's outside shoulder. You will see that it swings backward and forward. When the shoulder is back, the horse's leg is on the ground, and when the shoulder moves forward, the leg is raised. Time your posting to this shoulder movement, sitting down when the shoulder is back, and rising when the shoulder is forward. Your body will rise and fall with the horse's outside front leg.

If you wish to change the direction of your circle, or maybe make a figure eight, then you must also change your diagonal. All you need to do is sit down an extra beat of the trot as you make the turn to the new direction, so that you now rise on the other diagonal, once again on the outside of the circle.

CHAPTER 12

CANTERING AND GALLOPING

AT THE CANTER and the gallop, you are going to learn yet another new term, a "lead." If you stand in the middle of an arena and watch as a horse canters around you, you will notice that the two legs on the side of his body closest to you (called a lateral pair) strike the ground ahead of the outside pair. This is called being on the correct lead, and it is how the horse balances himself at a canter in a circle.

THE CANTER

At the canter, the rider once again goes back to the familiar basic position, sitting deep in the saddle with head and eyes up, shoulders back, and elbows in. Your seat should stay *in* the saddle, polishing it, and your hands (still some three inches above the withers) should move quietly with the rhythm of the horse's body.

Picking Up the Correct Lead   First, sit the trot. You will then have some forward momentum going and will be in the correct rider position for the canter. No matter which direction of the arena you are traveling, the basic canter aids are: sit up straight, shorten your reins, and squeeze your inside rein, at

The canter, with the horse on the correct lead, leading with the left (inside) lateral pair of legs.

the same time applying pressure behind the girth with your outside leg and *pushing* your seat down and forward into the saddle. This tells your horse that you want him to canter, striking off with the inside lateral pair of legs. This is easier said than done for the beginning rider, but if you conscientiously practice sitting up straight, giving the correct rein and leg aids, and pushing with your seat, you *will* succeed.

When you have mastered cantering on the correct lead from the sitting trot, try it from the walk. This is a little more difficult, because you are asking the horse to skip a gait, and go from a slow speed to a much faster one. To accomplish the canter from the walk, you will need very firm leg aids and an even stronger, driving seat. Once your horse is cantering, glance down with your eyes at the horse's shoulder on the inside of the circle you are making; you will easily be able to tell whether or not he is on the correct lead by watching his inside shoulder move forward, ahead of the outside shoulder.

What Is Cross-Firing?   This is also called a disunited canter. It occurs when the horse leads with the correct front leg but with the diagonal leg instead of the lateral hind leg following. If this ever happens to you, you will know immediately because your horse's canter suddenly becomes incredibly uncomfortable and impossible to ride.

What Is the Counter-Canter?   This means asking your horse to canter a circle on the wrong lead *intentionally.* It is a very advanced equitation test and should not be attempted by the beginner.

The gallop. Here the rider changes from the upright canter position to a forward position with seat out of the saddle and reins shortened.

THE GALLOP

The gallop is a larger and faster form of the canter, and you use the same aids to achieve the gallop as you use with the canter with perhaps a little more leg pressure. Once you are galloping, change your body position from the upright canter position to a forward position (called the half-seat), keeping your seat out of the saddle and standing in your stirrups. Your reins should be shortened so that you still maintain good contact with the horse's mouth. To slow down, straighten your back and brace your seat, while applying some pressure to the reins.

CHAPTER **13**

CLEANING UP AFTER YOU RIDE

ONE OF THE cardinal rules of horsemanship is to return your horse to the stable in a cool and calm condition. You can achieve this by walking him for the last half-hour of your ride, so that he arrives back at the stable relaxed and dry, not dripping with sweat. Allow plenty of time for cleaning up after your ride. You are going to have to untack your animal, cool him off, rub him down, and "put him up," which means putting him away. Additionally, you have your tack to clean and store. All these things seem to take much longer than planned, so it is a good idea to establish a cleanup routine for both horse and tack and stick to it each time you ride. Most horsemen love this part of their routine, because there is a special feeling of camaraderie between horse and rider after a ride together. This is the time to enhance your personal relationship with your horse.

UNTACKING

As soon as you dismount (on the near-side), link your arm through the rein, run up your stirrups, and loosen your girth. Next, unfasten the throatlatch and the noseband and remove the bridle, leaving only the reins around the neck while you put on the halter. Then hang your bridle up. Now turn your attention to the saddle. Undo the girth, put one hand on the

83

pommel, the other on the cantle, and gently slide both the saddle and pad toward you, folding the girth over the top of the saddle. Store your saddle in a safe place; you will clean it and the bridle later. First you must give your horse a rubdown to remove the dirt and sweat from his coat, and then put him up for the night.

COOLING OUT

In the wintertime, even though you religiously walk your horse slowly home, you may still arrive back at the stable with him steaming due to the long winter coat. You will have to walk the horse around the yard for an additional fifteen or twenty minutes, or until his body temperature feels normal to your touch, he has stopped steaming, and he appears relaxed. Now to the rubdown.

WINTERTIME RUBDOWN

In the winter you have to be especially conscientious about cooling off and rubbing down your horse. If the temperatures are frigid, obviously you cannot slosh cold water all over him; he could easily catch pneumonia. However, if you have access to hot water, then sponge his back and neck sparingly, drying him off thoroughly with your towel. If you don't have hot water, then just rub the wet coat with your dry towel or a straw wisp (a handful of straw or hay twisted into a pad). Rub the entire body hard to stir up the circulation to warm him up. Walk the horse around briskly if necessary. If he wears a blanket in the winter, place some straw under it when you put it on; in this way the warm air from the body can circulate and dry off the coat. Remove the straw when the coat is dry. Lastly, pick out your horse's feet.

SUMMERTIME RUBDOWN

Get a bucket of water and a large sponge and generously slosh the water over the dampened, sweaty parts of your horse's body—the neck, back, girth, chest, and between the back legs.

If you arrive back at the stable with a hot and steaming horse, then you must walk him around the yard for twenty minutes or so until his body temperature feels normal to your touch.

Then squeeze out your sponge and tenderly bathe around the eyes, behind the ears, and anywhere there are sweat marks on the face. Now get your sweat scraper, remove the excess water, and dry the horse off with your towel. When dry, brush out the water marks with your body brush. Lastly, pick out the feet.

PUTTING YOUR HORSE UP FOR THE NIGHT

Before you put your horse back in his field, paddock, or stall, take a good look at him. Does he appear relaxed and comfortable? Is the coat dry and clean? Have you cleaned out his feet? Have you remembered to put on his blanket if he wears one? If you can answer yes to all these questions, then you can return your horse to his quarters with a clear conscience.

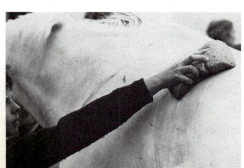

Generously slosh water over the sweaty parts of the horse's body, especially his back . . .

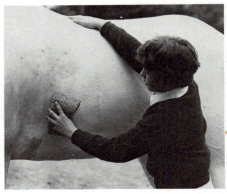

. . . and the girth area.

SAFETY FLASH! Don't leave your horse's halter on when you put him up. Halters can easily get caught on fencing, nails, even the horse's own rear shoe should he scratch his ear. More often than not, the halter doesn't break, the horse does. Avoid accidents and leave the halter conveniently outside the door or gate ready for you when you need it.

TACK CLEANING

Good-quality tack should last for years *if* it is properly and regularly cleaned. Not only is cleaning good for the leather, it also gives you the opportunity to check over your equipment piece by piece to make sure all leather, buckles, and stitching are intact.

To clean your tack, you will need a bar of glycerine soap (or any one of the many saddle soaps available), a sponge, and a bucket of clean water. For everyday quickie cleaning, all you need to do is hang up your bridle and park your saddle on a convenient rail or saddle rack; then go to work with your sponge, wrung out with clean water, removing dirt and sweat from the leather. Rinse the bit by dunking and sponging it off in your bucket of water; if you don't rinse the bit every time you ride, a hard, gritty scum soon forms around the edges that feels like harsh sandpaper in the horse's mouth. The next step is to go over the leather once again, this time with some of your saddle soap. This will leave your tack clean, soft, and with a pleasant, dull shine.

At least once a month, if not more, give your tack a complete

After every ride, the bridle should be cleaned with saddle soap and the bit rinsed off . . .

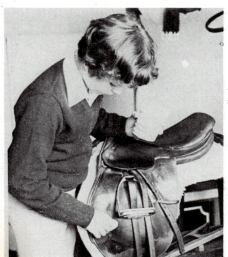

. . . and your saddle should be given a good cleaning.

stripdown clean. This means taking the bridle apart (remember where each piece goes, so that you can reassemble it correctly) and removing the girth, leathers, stirrups, and the pad from the saddle. Using a nondetergent liquid soap (such as Ivory) in some warm water, gently scrub the oily residue from each piece of leather with a soft nailbrush. Rinse each piece thoroughly in clear water and dry with a towel. Then apply saddle soap with a sponge, paying particular attention to the parts of the tack you missed when you were giving it a quickie clean, and allow it to completely sink in. Wash and then polish your bit and the stirrups, using a good-quality metal polish. Finally, reassemble the bridle and place the pad, girth, and stirrups back on the saddle.

Tack should be stored somewhere dry and dust-free. If possible, hang your bridle on a wooden dowel rather than a nail, as nails can eventually cause the headpiece of your bridle to crack. If you do not have a saddle horse or rack for your saddle, you can easily make one, using one large eyelet screwed into the wall and a piece of two-by-four-inch wood some eighteen inches long, with a hook screwed into one end. Simply insert the hook through the eyelet in the wall, and you have an instant saddle rack. When storing your saddle, cover it with a saddle cover or a clean towel and allow the pad to hang down, so that it can dry out completely between each ride.

At least once a month, give all your tack a complete stripdown clean.

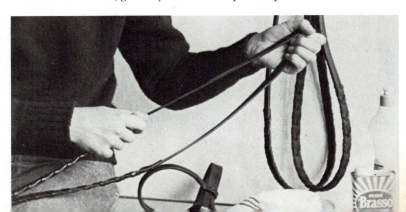

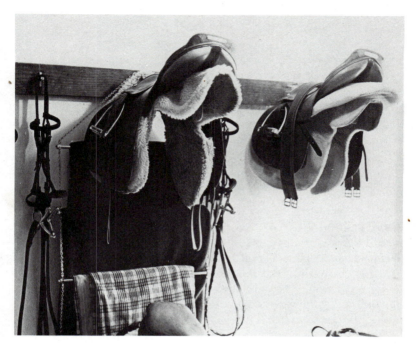

Tack should be stored somewhere dry and dust-free.

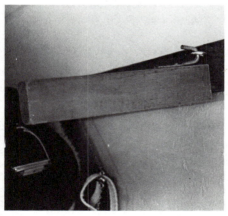

You can easily make a saddle rack for your saddle.

GLOSSARY

Aids   The various ways we communicate our requests to the horse.

Alfalfa   A legume hay, green in color.

Bridle   Leather harness that holds the bit in the horse's mouth.

Cantle   The back of the saddle.

Cavesson   The noseband of the bridle.

Chestnut   A golden-red coat color, or a horny growth on the inside of all horses' legs.

Conformation   The horse's physique.

Diagonals   The legs diagonally across the horse's body.

Eohippus   The earliest known ancestor of the modern horse.

Equestrian   A person who rides a horse.

Equitation   The art of riding horses.

Ergot   A small horny growth on the back of the fetlock joint.

Frog   The sensitive, triangular-shaped area on the underside of the horse's foot.

Gaits   The walk, trot, canter, and gallop. Also called paces.

Gelding   A castrated male horse.

Girth   The strap that passes under the belly to hold the saddle in place.

Green horse or rider   An inexperienced horse or rider.

Hand   The horse's height is measured in hands. Each hand is four inches.

Hay   Dried grasses and legumes; the horse's roughage.

Lateral pairs   The pair of legs on the same side of the horse's body.

Mare   An adult female horse.

Near-side   The left side of the horse.

Off-side   The right side of the horse.

Paddock   A fenced area used to house a horse; also used as a turn-out area.

Pommel   The raised arch at the front of the saddle.

Pony   Any equine under 14.2 hands.

Snaffle   A mild, jointed bit, with rings at each side.

Soundness   A horse that is not lame and shows no sign of disability.

Spur   A piece of equipment strapped to the heel of the rider's boot, which contains a shank used to touch the horse's sides. Spurs are worn on each boot. The spur is an artificial aid.

Stallion   An adult male horse, usually kept unaltered for breeding purposes. Also called a stud.

Stirrup   A device designed to hold the rider's foot; usually made of stainless steel.

Tack   All the riding equipment a horse wears.

Teeth floating   A method of rasping or filing down the horse's teeth to aid his digestion.

Thrush   A disease of the frog resulting in a foul-smelling black discharge.

Transitions   The changes between the various gaits as the horse moves from the walk through the trot and canter to the gallop, and back again to the halt.

Withers   A bony lump at the base of the horse's neck, behind which the saddle lies.

SUGGESTED FURTHER READING

British Horse Society. *The Manual of Horsemanship of the British Horse Society and The Pony Club.* New York: Barron's Educational Series, 1976.

Morris, George H. *George H. Morris Teaches Beginners to Ride.* New York: Doubleday, 1981.

Pervier, Evelyn. *The Beginning Rider: A Common Sense Approach.* New York: Julian Messner, 1980.

Stonebridge, M. A. *A Horse of Your Own.* New York: Doubleday, 1968.

Taylor, Louis. *Harper's Encyclopedia for Horsemen: The Complete Book of the Horse.* New York: Harper & Row, 1973.

INDEX

ABOUT THE AUTHOR

"I was born in England in 1936 and was horse crazed from infancy (to the amazement of my parents, who were not). In spite of the war and a total lack of funds, I somehow wangled my way into Pony Clubbing, exercising other people's horses. I was able to exercise racehorses later on. I came to the United States in 1959 and eventually married a saintly man who has patiently put up with my horse mania over the years. We have three children (two stepchildren and one of our own) and we live on a 200-acre ranch right on the Pacific Ocean, twenty miles north of San Francisco. Several years ago I started my own boarding stable, and I now take care of about forty-five horses. I also teach children to ride, put on horse shows, write articles, and take care of my family. I became an American citizen in 1967."